Tu-16 BADGER
in action

By Robert Bock

**Color by Don Greer
& Perry Manley**

Illustrated by Joe Sewell

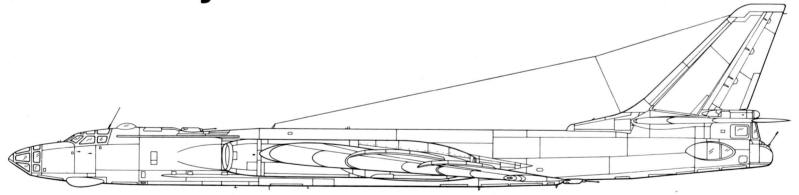

Aircraft Number 108

squadron/signal publications

A Soviet Naval Aviation (AV-MF) Tu-16 Badger D Maritime Reconnaissance/Electronic Warfare aircraft climbs to patrol altitude over the Pacific. The Badger D was the first of the electronic warfare Badgers.

ISBN 0-89747-252-7

If you have any photographs of the aircraft, armor, soldiers or ships of any nation, particularly wartime snapshots, why not share them with us and help make Squadron/Signal's books all the more interesting and complete in the future. Any photograph sent to us will be copied and the original returned. The donor will be fully credited for any photos used. Please send them to:

Squadron/Signal Publications, Inc.
1115 Crowley Drive.
Carrollton, TX 75011-5010.

Dedication

For my Mother and Father — thank you for everything.

Acknowledgments

I would like to thank my friends Marek Idzior and Andrzej Lesicki for their help and support in the writing of this book. A special thanks must also go to my wife, Kate, who was always understanding and forgiving, and to my children, Jan and Julia, who did not disturb me.

Photo Credits

Author's Collection
Swedish Air Force
U.S. Navy
Nicholas J. Waters III
Robert J. Ruffle

Military Photographic Agency
U.S. Department of Defense
Larry Davis
Lee Thomas
Bill Strandberg

Editor's Note

The name Badger is not actually part of the Soviet designation of the Tu-16. Badger is in fact a NATO Reporting Name; that is, a name assigned to the aircraft by the North Atlantic Treaty Organization's Air Standards Co-ordinating Committee, a joint committee made up of members from all NATO countries. The purpose of these reporting names is to allow rapid radio identification/reporting of Soviet aircraft types. The names are all designed to sound different so that they will not be confused, even under conditions of poor radio reception.

Single syllable names are used for propeller driven aircraft, while multiple syllable names are used for jet powered aircraft. The name also gives the basic mission of the aircraft. Names beginning with F are for fighters, transports all begin with C, helicopters with H, and miscellaneous types (trainers, reconnaissance, etc.) begin with M.

Bomber aircraft all have names beginning with B, therefore under the NATO Reporting Name System, the Tu-16 was named Badger indicating that it is a jet powered bomber aircraft. Variants of the basic aircraft are all identified by a suffix letter. The second Tu-16 variant identified by NATO would receive the name Badger B, the third Badger C, etc. Often this does not follow actual Soviet production. As an example, a type may actually be a third production variant, and be identified/named by NATO before the second production variant was seen by NATO observers.

A U.S. Navy A-7E Corsair II escorts a Tu-16 Badger E away from a Navy task group in the Pacific during April of 1984. Badger overflights are common during Navy exercises, especially if a carrier task group is involved.

3

INTRODUCTION

On 27 October 1937, agents of the infamous NKVD arrested Andrey Nikoayevich Tupolev on the charge of being a "Class Enemy" who had provided Willy Messerschmitt with plans for an aircraft quite similar to the Bf-110. At the same time a group of other aviation designers and engineers including V. Petlakov, V. Myasishchev and A. Putilov were also arrested and put into Butyrka Prison.

Tupolev spent almost a year in prison till Lavrentii Beria recalled that there were a large number of aviation designers/engineers in prison and/or labor camps. Beria envisioned the establishment of a special Design Bureau designated the TsKB-29 NKVD using the talents of these prisoners. The bureau was also called *Spetstekhotdel*, or Special Technical Detachment. Later the name was once more changed to STO (from the Russian word for One Hundred). As a result, aircraft designed by the Bureau were designated 100, 102, 103, 110, etc. Among the 150 members of this design bureau were six future members of the Soviet Academy of Sciences, twelve professors and assistant professors, seventeen chief designers and other aviation specialists.

While in prison, Tupolev designed what was perhaps the best Soviet bomber of the Second World War. Originally known as Aircraft 103, the aircraft was later redesignated as the Tu-2. After the outbreak of the Second World War, Stalin was forced to look for ways to strengthen the Red Army and Air Force. Imprisoned military officers were released, as were the members of the STO. Tupolev was set free on 27 July 1941. His bomber, however, had been taken out of production so that available factory space could be used to produce Yakovlev Yak 7 fighters. The Yak 7 received production priority as a result of the political efforts of A.S. Yakovlev, who had taken full advantage of his position as the deputy minister for the aviation industry.

Yakovlev was also partially responsible for the decision that ended production of strategic bombers for the Soviet Air Force (VVS) throughout the war years. When the war drew to a close, the Soviets found that they did not have a true strategic bomber in service. With the introduction of nuclear weapons, the importance of heavy strategic bombers increased significantly. Although it had been decided to develop long range missiles as the primary platform for Soviet nuclear power, introduction of these vehicles was still a long way off and until they could be developed, only a long range strategic heavy bomber could carry a nuclear bomb over the distances required.

The solution to the bomber problem appeared as if by luck. On 29 July 1944, a Boeing B-29-5-BW (42-6256) Superfortress piloted by CAPT Howard R. Jarrell was damaged by anti-aircraft fire during an attack on the Showa Steel Works at Ashan. Unable to make it back to home base, Jarrell headed the B-29 toward the Soviet Union and landed on the small airfield at Tarrichanka. After weeks of interrogation, Jarrell and his crew were sent to an internment camp in Turkestan.

Three weeks later, a second Superfortress, B-29A-1-BN (42-93829), crashed near Khabarovsk. Finally, during November of 1944, a third B-29-5-BW (serial 42-6358) fell into Soviet hands. These three B-29s, at the time the most advanced production bomber in the world, became the prototypes of a new Soviet strategic bomber. With the B-29s available to serve as pattern aircraft, the Russians abandoned several designs (among them Tupolev's Design 64) and concentrated on copying the American B-29.

It was not a simple task. Even without the difficulty of converting all the American measurements to the metric system, the Soviet aviation industry was completely unprepared to take advantage of the advanced technology in the Superfortress. Tupolev's team was assigned the task of copying and adapting the B-29 airframe, while A. B. Shvetsov's bureau was to copy the Wright-Cyclone R-3350 engine. Other teams were occupied in copying the aircraft's electronics, armament and other systems.

The Superfortress was copied in an incredibly short period of time and, on 3 August 1947, three new B-29s wearing Red star markings flew over the spectators on Moscow's Red Square during a military display. These were the first three aircraft of a twenty aircraft pre-production batch produced by Tupolev under the designation Tu-4 (NATO reporting name Bull). These aircraft were almost identical to the B-29, differing mainly in having the pressurized crew compartments built as separate sections without a connecting tunnel.

Over the course of Tu-4 production the defensive armament was strengthened. Initially, the Tu-4s were produced with an armament of ten 12.7MM machine guns. These were changed to 20MM cannons and still later to 23MM weapons. The Tu-4 became the standard bomber for Soviet long-range aviation throughout the late 1940s. It was also used as a tanker, cargo transport (Tu-75), paratroop carrier (Tu-4T) and reconnaissance aircraft (Tu-4R) equipped with additional fuel tanks and cameras mounted in the bomb bay.

During the late 1940s, it became obvious that the Tu-4 needed to be replaced. It was far too slow and its range fell short of being truly intercontinental. Since it was the end of the Second World War, a new political order has been established. Two opposing political and military centers had become dominant — America and the Soviet Union. The Americans were in a better military position, since they had the advantage of numerous bases surrounding the USSR. The Russians could only reach targets in the U.S. from bases within their own territory. For this reason the Russians spent vast amounts of funds on the development of intercontinental missiles and long range bombers.

Tupolev tried to improve the Tu-4, especially in its range. Successive modifications, designated Designs 80 and 85, were built. These retained many components of the Tu-4 but were characterized by larger wing spans, increased fuel capacity, improved aerodynamics and more powerful engines. The final variant, known as the Design 85 (NATO reporting name Barge) had a thirty percent greater wing span than the Tu-4 and a range of 7,200 km (4,474 miles). A further modification to the Design 85 saw the aircraft re-engined with four M-35 engines. This aircraft was to have carried a 5,000 kg (11,022 pounds) bomb load at a distance of 17,000 km (10,563 miles). The project, however, was never put into production, being superseded by the Design 95.

The swept wing Design 95 was powered by four 12,000 shp NK-12 turboprop engines with counter-rotating propellers. After successful testing, Design 95 was introduced into the Soviet strategic air forces under the service designation Tu-95 (NATO reporting name Bear). This aircraft has seen years of successful service and, some thirty years after its maiden flight, was reinstated into production as the Tu-142M (NATO reporting name Bear H) armed with the AS-15 Kent cruise missiles.

This was one of three Boeing B-29s that fell into Soviet hands during the Second World War. The aircraft was named *Ding How* and carried the serial number 28358 (USAAF serial 42-6358). It is unclear if the Soviets repainted the number in error or changed the 6 to 8 purposely.

On 17 December 1947, the American Boeing B-47 Stratojet made its maiden flight and Tupolev was pressed to speed up work on several new jet bomber projects. During 1949, Tupolev started construction of Design 83, but the project was abandoned before the prototype was completed. During this same time period, the preliminary sketches of three new designs, (86, 88 and 90) appeared on Tupolev's drawing board.

Tupolev initially proposed the three different designs to replace the Tu-4. All three featured the same fuselage design, differing mainly in the engines. Design 86 was to have been equipped with the Mikulin AM-TRD-02 (TR-3) engines in underwing gondolas. The engines proved unreliable and underpowered, causing Tupolev to abandon the aircraft. Design 90 was also abandoned because of problems with its engines (NK-12 turboprops).

Tupolev had preferred Design 88 (also referred to as the the Type N for security reasons) and decided to go ahead with development of this aircraft. Design 88 was designed to use the powerful 19,290 pounds thrust (lbst) AM-03 turbojet engine built by the Mikulin OKB. Dmitrii S. Markov was appointed as project chief engineer with Tupolev supervising all work on the project.

Tupolev was not satisfied with the early fuselage design because its wide cross-section. Eventually, Tupolev designed an area rule, narrow diameter cylindrical shaped fuselage with the engines semi-recessed along the fuselage sides. The diameter of the fuselage was partially determined by the diameter of the largest Soviet bomb, the FAB-9000, which was to be carried in the bomb bay.

Wind tunnel testing of the Design 88 in the TsAGI T-101 wind tunnel showed that the design was very clean with a very low drag. During the early 1950s there were many advocates of the wing root engine installation mainly because of its low drag and the fact that it left the swept wings aerodynamically clean. The wing of Design 88 was not "completely" clean. In the space where the engines would normally be mounted, Tupolev mounted large pods to house the landing gear. The final landing gear design was proposed by team member A.A. Yudin and it consisted of a four bogie main wheel landing gear housed in the wing pods which extended back past the wing trailing edge.

The Design 88 prototype made its first flight on 27 April 1952 with experimental test pilot N.S. Rybko at the controls. State trials were conducted by B. N. Grozdov, while I. A. Starkov was responsible for factory test. While the factory trials were quickly completed, it was six months before the state acceptance trials were finished. During testing the Design 88 prototype achieved a maximum speed of 945 km/h (587 mph) and a ceiling of 11,000 meters (36,000 feet).

In December of 1952, the Soviet government decided to place the Design 88 into production despite its slow speed and inadequate range. Tupolev did not agree with this decision, because in his opinion the aircraft was far too heavy (80,000 kg/176,366 pounds). He proposed a new variant which was lighter by some 5,500 kg (12,125 pounds) and convinced the government to change its first decision.

The modified bomber received the service designation Tu-16 and the second prototype made its maiden flight during 1953 while preparations for series production continued. The Tu-16 prototype had far better performance than its predecessor: speed was now 992 kmh (616 mph), ceiling was 12,800 meters (41,995 feet), range was 5,760 km (3,579 miles) with a bomb load of 3,000 kg (6,614 pounds) and the aircraft's weight had dropped to 72,000 kg (158,730 pounds).

Full production of the Tu-16 began during early 1954. The first nine aircraft were revealed to the public on 1 May 1954 and it received the NATO reporting name Badger.

The second Tu-16 prototype shares the airfield with a number of Tu-4 Bull bombers. The aircraft had the official OKB number 88 and was also known as the Type N for security reasons. The aircraft was overall natural metal with no markings other than the national insignia.

Development

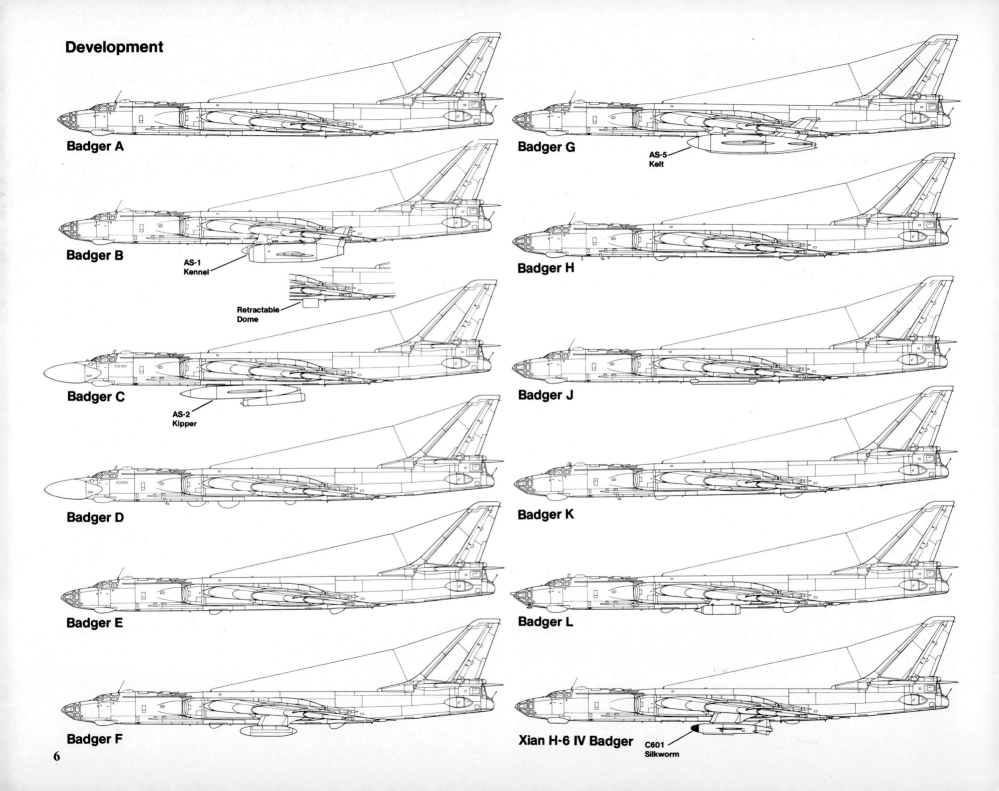

Badger A

Badger B
AS-1
Kennel

Retractable
Dome

Badger C
AS-2
Kipper

Badger D

Badger E

Badger F

Badger G
AS-5
Kelt

Badger H

Badger J

Badger K

Badger L

Xian H-6 IV Badger
C601
Silkworm

Tu-16 Badger A

The production Tu-16 differed little from the prototype except in the position of the pitot tubes on the nose, the shape of the main landing gear doors, and in the types of antennas carried. The main landing gear doors were changed with the single piece front opening door being deleted in favor of two piece side opening doors. The two pitot/air sensor tubes on the nose under the cockpit were repositioned and the single blade antenna in front of the cockpit was changed to a three pole IFF antenna (NATO reporting name Odd Rods).

The production Tu-16 was a classic level bomber which was given the NATO reporting name Badger A. The aircraft was equipped with an internal bomb bay mounted in the fuselage between the engines. This bay was large enough to house an FAB-9000 bomb (although the bomb protruded slightly from the bomb bay) or a combination of smaller bombs up to a total of 9,000 kg (19,942 pounds).

Defensive armament for the Tu-16 Badger A consisted of three remote controlled gun turrets (dorsal, ventral and tail) each armed with twin 23MM NR-23 cannons. Additionally, a single fixed NR-23 cannon was mounted on the starboard side of the nose just behind the bombardier's position and fired by the pilot. For navigational purposes and blind bombing, a PRS-1 AG Argon bomb/nav radar was mounted in a streamlined radome on the underside of the fuselage just behind the navigator/bombardier's compartment.

The crew compartments consisted of a pressurized compartment in the nose and a second pressurized compartment in the tail for the two rear gunners. In the prototype, these compartments were connected by a tunnel, however, this feature was deleted on production Tu-16s. Entry to the two compartments was made through three hatches in the fuselage underside: one on the nose, and two at the rear of the aircraft.

It is believed that most of the 2,000 Tu-16s produced were the basic Badger A bomber airframe, with the superseding variants being remanufactured/modified Badger As. Late production Badger As differed from early batches in having lengthened wing airflow fences, an enlarged chin radome and in the positioning of various windows and hatches.

One modified Tu-16 Badger A (Serial 4201002) was tested between 1954-55 with a greatly increased fuel capacity. This increased the gross weight from 71,560 kg to 75,800 kg which caused takeoff speed to rise from 280 kmh to 288 kmh and the takeoff run to go from 1,900 to 2,180 meters (7,152 feet). After successful testing, this new configuration was cleared for production, allowing Badger A bombers to carry significantly more fuel with the same bomb load.

Another modification that occurred early during Badger A production was the replacement of the 8,750 kg (19,290 lbst) AM-3 engines with more powerful 9,500 kg (20,944 lbst) AM-3M engines (these engines were redesignated, RD-3M, when Sergiey Tumanski became the OKB chief after Alexander Mikulin was dismissed for misconduct). The re-engined Tu-16 Badger A had a top speed of 1,050 kmh (652 mph), a ceiling of 15,000 meters (49,213 feet) and a range of 7,200 km (4,474 miles).

Although externally identical to the Tu-16 Badger A, a dedicated atomic bomb carrier, the Tu-16A, was built as a modification of the basic Tu-16 airframe. Another modification was the Tu-16T, a torpedo bomber with a modified bomb bay, which could house four RAT-52 torpedos, two WB-2F guided bombs, twelve AMD-500 mines or four AMD-1000 mines. Again, this aircraft was externally identical to the standard Tu-16 Badger A and no new NATO name was assigned.

The Tu-16 Badger A on display at Monino has a large Blue 50 painted on the nose. Aircraft attached to combat units had their tactical number on the tail and nosewheel doors. The astrodome behind the cockpit was used by a gunner who operated the remote control dorsal turret.

There are reports that Soviet Badger As have participated in combat operations during the Afghan war. Tu-16s of the VVS reportedly carried out medium level bombing attacks against targets in Afghanistan from their bases across the border in Uzbekistan, although it is believed that there were only a small number of such operations.

Tu-16N Tanker

A number of TU-16 Badger A bombers were converted to the aerial tanker role by mounting a fuel tank in the bomb bay and installing a refueling hose system in the starboard wingtip This system is unique and requires the receiver aircraft to engage the trailing hose with its port wingtip. Once engaged, the fuel flow is begun and it is estimated that refueling by this method requires some ten to fifteen minutes to complete.

Later tanker variants of the Tu-16N discarded the wingtip hose for a hose and drogue refueling method, similar to that used by the U.S. Navy. The hose/basket is stowed in the bomb bay of the Badger A tanker and reeled out to be engaged by the probe of the receiver aircraft (such as Tu-22 Blinder, Tu-95 Bear and Tu-22M Backfire bombers).

The remote controlled ventral gun barbette was armed with two NR-23 23ᴍᴍ cannons with 700 rounds per gun. The guns can depress 95°, elevate 2°, and rotate a full 360°.

Nose Development

Tu-16 Prototype

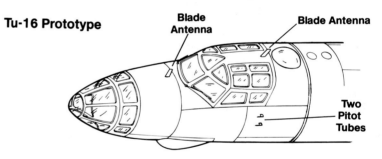

Blade Antenna

Blade Antenna

Two Pitot Tubes

Tu-16 Badger A

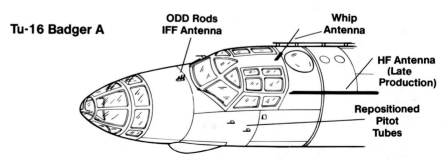

ODD Rods IFF Antenna

Whip Antenna

HF Antenna (Late Production)

Repositioned Pitot Tubes

The navigator/bombardier of the Tu-16 Badger A was housed in the glazed nose section and manned the RBP-4 Rubin 1 bomb sight which was mounted behind a optically flat armor glass panel. The panel under the nose is the navigator/bombardier entry hatch.

A Tu-16 Badger A drops a load of twelve 1,102 pound bombs during armament testing. The Badger A was used as a level bomber in combat during the Afghanistan war where they were deployed in bombing attacks on the cities of Herat and Kandshan.

Main Landing Gear Door

Tu-16 Prototype

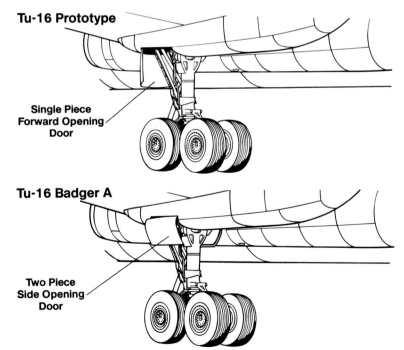

Single Piece Forward Opening Door

Tu-16 Badger A

Two Piece Side Opening Door

The rear compartment was occupied by the rear turret gunner who operated the rear turret guns and PRS-1 radar gun sight and an observer/gunner who operated the under fuselage turret. The under fuselage turret was sighted by using the two large blister windows below the horizontal stabilizers.

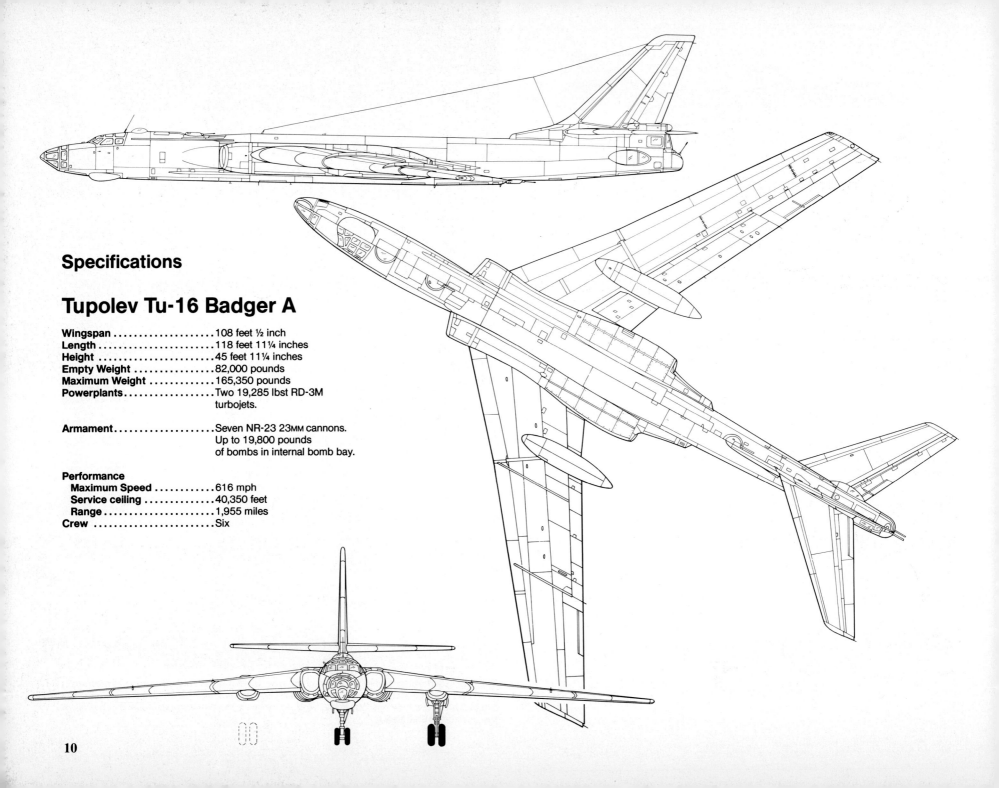

Specifications

Tupolev Tu-16 Badger A

Wingspan	108 feet ½ inch
Length	118 feet 11¼ inches
Height	45 feet 11¼ inches
Empty Weight	82,000 pounds
Maximum Weight	165,350 pounds
Powerplants	Two 19,285 lbst RD-3M turbojets.
Armament	Seven NR-23 23ᴍᴍ cannons. Up to 19,800 pounds of bombs in internal bomb bay.

Performance
Maximum Speed	616 mph
Service ceiling	40,350 feet
Range	1,955 miles
Crew	Six

An F/A-18 Hornet escorts a pair of Badgers over the Mediterranean Sea. The Badger in the foreground is a Badger J ECM aircraft while the aircraft in the background is a Badger A tanker.

A Tu-16N Badger A (left) tanker passes fuel to a Tu-16R Badger E (right). The two ventral radomes on the Tu-16R house passive electronic reconnaissance equipment and the bomb bay carries a pallet with cameras.

A Tu-16R Badger E reconnaissance aircraft takes on fuel from a Tu-16N Badger A tanker. The White rectangle on the side of the Tu-16N, just behind the jet exhaust, is a visual reference point for the pilot of the aircraft being refueled.

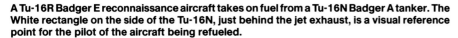

During refueling operations the gunner/radio operator, who mans the rear compartment side observation blisters under the tail, is responsible for guiding the pilot. This crewman also serves as the lead gunner, commanding all gun stations during combat.

11

Missile Carriers

Tu-16KS-1 Badger B

To meet the needs of the Soviet Naval Air Arm (AV-MF) for a stand-off anti-ship missile carrier, Tupolev modified the basic Tu-16 aircraft to carry two KS-1 (NATO reporting name AS-1 Kennel) air-to-surface cruise missiles under the designation Tu-16KS-1. This Badger variant was first revealed to the West during 1961 and received the NATO reporting name Badger B.

Internally, there is little difference between the Tu-16KS-1 Badger B and the standard Tu-16 Badger A, with both aircraft being equipped with a bomb bay for level bombing. There are some avionics and electronics differences, with the Badger B being equipped with the Komet III I band radar in addition to the standard bomb/nav radar. Externally, the Badger B differed from the Badger A in having a missile pylon under each wing capable of carrying a single KS-1 (AS-1) missile, and in the addition of a small window on the port fuselage side near the engine air intake. The KS-1 *Kryliatyi Snariad* was designed by the Mikoyan OKB. It was a small pilotless aircraft similar in appearance to the MiG-15 fighter. It was powered by an RD-500 turbojet engine, had a top speed of 1,200 kph (745 mph), a range of 200 km (124 miles) and was armed with a 900 kg (1,984 pound) high explosive warhead.

The missile was guided by data link corrections supplied by the Komet III radar housed in a retractable radome under the Badger B's center fuselage. Missile terminal homing was accomplished by a small onboard radar mounted in the missile's nose. Operationally, the Badger B's assigned mission was anti-shipping strike, with its primary target being the aircraft carriers of the U.S. Navy.

Besides seeing service with the Soviet Navy, at least twenty Tu-16KS-1 Badger Bs were supplied to the Indonesian Air Force (TNI-AU) where they equipped two squadrons, Nos 41 and 42. These aircraft were active during the Indonesian confrontation with Malaysia, flying sorties into Malaysian airspace near Singapore. The Indonesian Badgers remained active until they were forced out of service by a lack of spare parts.

When the KS-1 became obsolete, many Badger Bs had their missile pylons removed and the aircraft reverted to the conventional level bombing role, while others were converted to carry later missiles.

Ground crewmen maneuver a KS-1 air-to-surface cruise missile (NATO code name AS-1 Kennel) on its handling dolly. The missile is carried on a pylon under the wing of the Tu-16KS-1 Badger B. After the KS-1 was withdrawn from service, Badger Bs reverted to the bomber role.

The Tu-16KS-1 Badger B was equipped to carry two Kennel air-to-surface cruise missiles on underwing pylons. The aircraft was overall Natural Metal with the tactical number, 62, in Red on the tail and on each nosewheel door.

A Tu-16KS-1 Badger B fires an AS-1 Kennel air-to-surface missile from its starboard wing pylon. The Badger B carried a large retractable radome in the bomb bay that housed the guidance radar for the AS-1.

Fuselage Development

Tu-16
Badger A

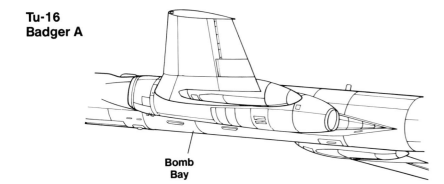

Bomb
Bay

Tu-16KS-1
Badger B

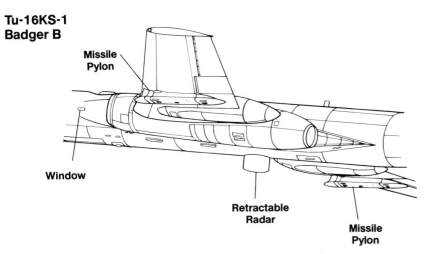

Missile
Pylon

Window

Retractable
Radar

Missile
Pylon

This Tu-16KS-1 Badger B served with the Indonesian Air Force during the early 1960s. The aircraft were routinely flown armed with a pair of AS-1 Kennel missiles. The retractable missile guidance radome is deployed on this aircraft.

A Tu-16KS-1 Badger B of the Indonesian Air Force (TNI-AU) parked on a taxiway at an Indonesian Air Force Base. After the break in relations between Indonesia and the Soviet Union, support for the Badgers was withdrawn. The aircraft were soon out of service due to a lack of spare parts.

13

Tu-16K-10 Badger C

As the KS-1 missile became outdated and was superseded by larger, heavier, more powerful cruise missiles, the Tu-16 was further modified to serve as the launching platform for the next generation of stand-off weapons.

The next cruise missile to enter service was the K-10 (NATO reporting name AS-2 Kipper), a supersonic, anti-ship weapon. To be able to carry and provide guidance for the K-10, a number of modifications to the basic Tu-16 airframe were necessary. These resulted in the next variant of the Badger, the Tu-16K-10 known to NATO as the Badger C.

The K-10/AS-2 Kipper was almost ten meters (32 feet) long and weighed 4,500 kg/9,920 pounds (including a 1,000 kg/2,204 pound warhead). It was powered by the RD-9 turbojet engine giving it supersonic speed and a range of 250 km (155 miles). The missile was carried under the fuselage of the Tu-16K-10, semi-recessed in the bomb bay.

To mount a radar powerful enough to guide the K-10 over its entire range, the glass nose of the Tu-16 Badger A was replaced with a large, flat radome. This radome housed the target acquisition/guidance radar (NATO reporting name Puff Ball). In an attack, the K-10 is guided to the target by a preprogrammed autopilot with updates from the launching Badger C radar. When it nears the target area, the Tu-16K-10 issues command guidance instructions and illuminates the target with the Puff Ball. In the terminal phase of the attack, the missile is guided by its onboard radar.

Other modifications to the Badger C include the addition of two small windows on the fuselage side just behind and below the cockpit and the addition of two small raked back blade antennas to the fuselage underside forward of the bomb bay.

Badger C Modified

The Tu-16 Badger C Modified differed from the standard Badger C in the addition of wing pylons (identical to those mounted on the Badger B) for carrying two supersonic AS-6 (NATO reporting name Kingfish) anti-ship missiles.

A Tu-16K-10 Badger C in flight over the Pacific ocean near a U.S. Navy battle group during 1984. The Badger C had two additional small windows in the fuselage side just under the cockpit. The aircraft's tactical number revealed that it was assigned to the Second Squadron within the Regiment.

A pair of Tu-16K-10 Badger Cs, armed with AS-2 Kipper air-to-surface missiles, conduct a low level flyby during the 1961 Tushino Air Show. The Badger C was the first variant to be equipped with the large nose radome for the Puff Ball radar.

A Tu-16K-10 Badger C launches an AS-2 Kipper air-to-surface missile. This aircraft has been modified with the Towel Rail aerial, usually carried on the starboard side, relocated to the port fuselage side in the location normally occupied by the long HF blade antenna.

Nose Development

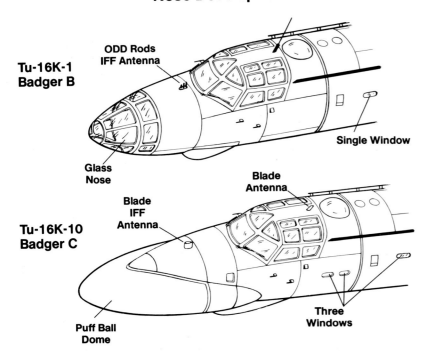

Tu-16K-1 Badger B

ODD Rods IFF Antenna

Single Window

Glass Nose

Tu-16K-10 Badger C

Blade Antenna

Blade IFF Antenna

Puff Ball Dome

Three Windows

The AS-2 was carried semi-recessed in the weapons bay of the Badger C. The small dark circle in front of the Red missile is the viewing window for a vertical strike camera. The aircraft's tactical number is repeated on both nosewheel doors.

15

This Tu-16KS-10 Badger C Modified is on a training/reconnaissance flight with all weapons bays and pylons empty. The underwing missile pylons fitted on various Badgers are of the same design regardless of the variant.

This Badger C Modified is carrying two two AS-6 Kingfish missiles on the under wing pylons and an AS-2 Kipper under the fuselage. The Badger C is the only Tu-16 variant that can carry the Kipper missile.

A Tu-16 Badger C Mod takes on fuel from a Tu-16N Badger A tanker. The small drogue parachute used to stabilize the fuel hose is visible just behind the wingtip of the Badger C Mod. Both aircraft are overall Natural Metal with Black numbers.

This Badger C carries an Excellent Aircraft award in Red under the cockpit. Badger Cs are in service with all Soviet Naval Air Fleets: Black Sea, Baltic, Northern and Pacific. This aircraft is carrying multiple ejector type bomb racks under the fuselage.

Fuselage Development

**Tu-16K-1
Badger B**

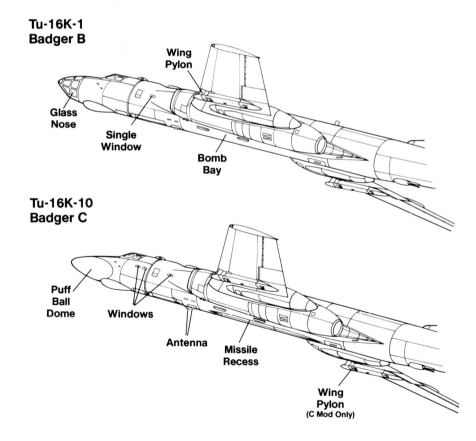

Glass Nose
Single Window
Wing Pylon
Bomb Bay

**Tu-16K-10
Badger C**

Puff Ball Dome
Windows
Antenna
Missile Recess
Wing Pylon
(C Mod Only)

A Tu-16KS-10 Badger C Modified of the Soviet Navy. The aircraft is carrying an AS-6 Kingfish on the port wing pylon. The recess in the bomb bay door is the missile well for carrying the AS-5 Kipper cruise missile.

This pair of Badger Cs are both carrying under fuselage bomb racks (visible just under the engine intakes) in addition to their normal wing pylons for AS-6 cruise missiles.

17

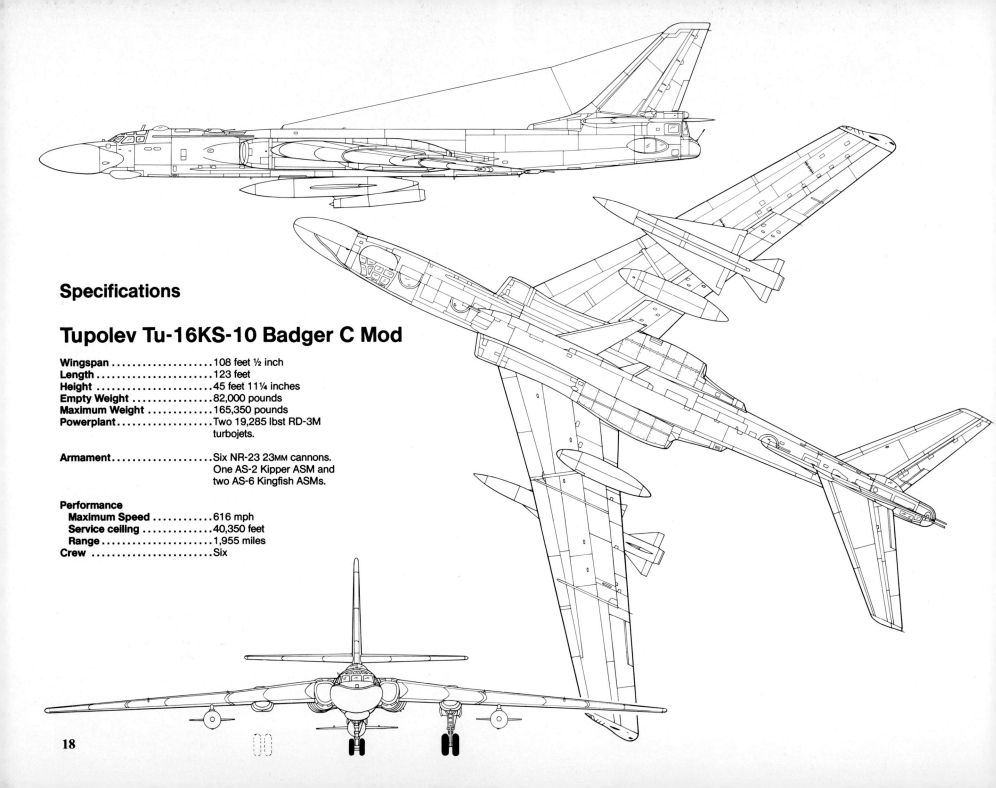

Specifications

Tupolev Tu-16KS-10 Badger C Mod

Wingspan .108 feet ½ inch
Length . . . . .123 feet
Height . . . . .45 feet 11¼ inches
Empty Weight . . . . .82,000 pounds
Maximum Weight . . . . .165,350 pounds
Powerplant . . . . .Two 19,285 lbst RD-3M
　　　　　　　　　　　　　　　　turbojets.

Armament . . . . .Six NR-23 23мм cannons.
　　　　　　　　　　　　　　　　One AS-2 Kipper ASM and
　　　　　　　　　　　　　　　　two AS-6 Kingfish ASMs.

Performance
　Maximum Speed . . . . .616 mph
　Service ceiling . . . . .40,350 feet
　Range . . . . .1,955 miles
Crew . . . . .Six

This Badger C is carrying bomb racks fitted to the missile pylons and has been modified with additional blade communications antennas above and below the fuselage.

This Badger C is dropping a bomb load from racks fitted to the underwing missile pylons. The racks are believed to be capable of carrying four bombs or mines giving the Badger a total external load of eight free fall weapons.

Air-to-Surface Missiles

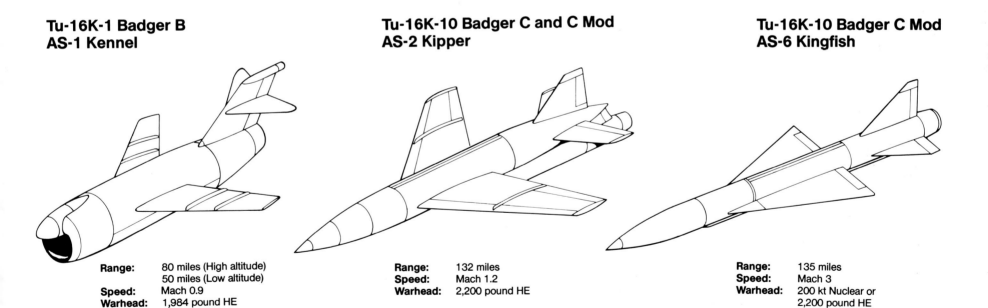

Tu-16K-1 Badger B
AS-1 Kennel

Range:	80 miles (High altitude)
	50 miles (Low altitude)
Speed:	Mach 0.9
Warhead:	1,984 pound HE

Tu-16K-10 Badger C and C Mod
AS-2 Kipper

Range:	132 miles
Speed:	Mach 1.2
Warhead:	2,200 pound HE

Tu-16K-10 Badger C Mod
AS-6 Kingfish

Range:	135 miles
Speed:	Mach 3
Warhead:	200 kt Nuclear or
	2,200 pound HE

Tu-16 Badger G

When the AS-5 (NATO reporting name Kelt) was introduced into service during 1968, a decision was made to arm the Badger with these updated and improved missiles. Externally identical to the earlier Badger B (and believed to be rebuilt from Badger B airframes) the Kelt missile carrier was first identified by NATO during September of 1968 and given the reporting name Badger G. The Badger G carried two AS-5s while retaining its free fall bombing capability. The main difference between the Badger B and Badger G, besides the missiles, was in the radar carried by the Badger G. The Argon nav/bombing radar was replaced by a long range target acquisition radar (NATO reporting name Short Horn).

The AS-5 Kelt was powered by a liquid fuel rocket engine and was equipped with an improved guidance system. The AS-5 is armed with a 2,200 pound warhead and employs a preprogrammed autopilot with command updates and active radar terminal homing. The missile has a speed of Mach 1.2 and a range of 200 miles. It is estimated that, as of 1976, about 1,000 Kelt missiles have been produced.

Just before the outbreak of the June 1967 Six-Day Arab-Israeli War, the Egyptian Air Force had on strength some twenty Tu-16KS-1 Badger Bs. These Badgers were destroyed during the first few hours of the war and none took part in the fighting. After the war, the Soviets quickly replaced the Egyptian losses with another twenty Tu-16s. These aircraft were Badger Gs armed with two AS-5 Kelt missiles.

During the course of the October 1973 Yom Kippur War, Egyptian Tu-16 Badger Gs launched some twenty-five Kelt missiles against Israeli targets. Most of these were shot down by Israeli fighters and anti-aircraft defenses. Only five hit their targets, destroying two radar stations and a supply dump in the Sinai. One Tu-16 was shot down during the war. At present Egypt possesses some sixteen Tu-16s which are assigned to the bomber brigade based in the southern part of the country.

After the break in relations between Egypt and the Soviet Union on 14 March 1976, the Soviets cut off the supply of spare parts for Soviet equipment including the Tu-16s. As a result, Egypt turned to China. According to an agreement signed during April of 1976, Egypt was supplied with spare parts for the Chinese built Tu-16 variant, the H-6 bomber. Reportedly, part of the deal included the exchange of modern Soviet military equipment to China including at least one MiG-23BN Flogger F fighter-bomber.

A number of Badger Gs and AS-5 Kelt missiles were also supplied to the Iraqi Air Force where they have seen combat. Reportedly, Iraqi Badgers were used to launch AS-5 attacks against Iranian targets during the early phases of the Iran/Iraq war.

Badger G Modified

During December of 1977, a Japanese Air Self Defense Force F-86 fighter pilot took a photograph of a Tu-16 Badger G armed with a new missile on its underwing pylon. This missile was later identified as the AS-6 (NATO reporting name Kingfish). With the change in missile armament came a change in the NATO reporting name, with these Badger Gs now being referred to as the Badger G Modified or, more commonly, the Badger G Mod.

A Badger G, armed with an AS-5 Kelt air-to-surface anti-ship cruise missile, flies over the ocean. The Badger G replaced the Badger B in the missile carrier role.

Since that time, the AS-6 armed Badger G Mod has gradually replaced the Badger G/AS-5 combination in Soviet Naval service. The AS-6 is powered by a liquid fuel rocket motor giving the weapon a speed of Mach 3. The missile has a range of 200 km (124 miles) at low level or 500 km (310 miles) at altitude. It is guided by a autopilot with mid-course correction (via data link) and terminal radar homing. The Kingfish can be armed with a conventional 1,000 kg (2,200 pounds) explosive warhead or a nuclear weapon.

The Badger G Modified armed with one or two AS-6 missiles (depending on mission duration) has become the basic strike variant of the Badger in Soviet Naval service. To maintain a constant level flight attitude prior to missile launch, the Badger G Mod has a small inverted T-shape device on the nose just above the bombardier's station. Additionally, a number of Badger G Mods have had the nose mounted Short Horn radar replaced by a larger radome mounted on the fuselage underside just in front of the weapons bay.

A Tu-16 Badger G missile carrier armed with two AS-5 Kelt air-to-surface cruise missiles on its underwing pylons. In addition to the missile armament, the Badger G retained its level bombing capability.

A Tu-16N tanker (background) delivers its load of fuel to a Badger G missile carrier (foreground). The tail bumper of the Badger G is down while the tanker has its bumper retracted. The fin tips are painted different colors; the missile carrier has a White tip while the tanker has a Green tip.

Crews of an AV MF (Naval Aviation) regiment head for their aircraft in preparation for another over water training/reconnaissance flight. For these missions, the Badger Gs normally do not carry their missile armament. The aircraft are overall natural metal with the tactical number repeated on the tail and both nosewheel doors.

The starboard missile pylon of a Tu-16 Badger G. The various missiles carried by Tu-16s have one thing in common — they are all carried on underwing pylons of the same shape and construction.

This Badger G carries an inverted T shaped device mounted above the bombardier/navigator's position. It is believed that this device is used to assist the pilot in maintaining a level flight attitude prior to launching the AS-6 Kingfish missile.

The inverted T shaped sensor on the nose of this Badger G Mod is believed to be used to help the pilot maintain a level flight attitude prior to missile launch. The chin radome houses a Short Horn search and missile guidance radar.

Nose Development

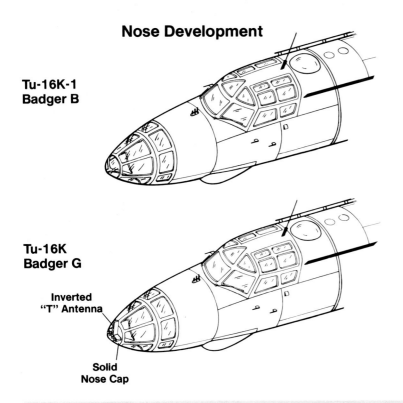

**Tu-16K-1
Badger B**

**Tu-16K
Badger G**

Inverted
"T" Antenna

Solid
Nose Cap

This Egyptian Air Force Badger Gs carries a large tactical number on the forward fuselage and Arabic style numbers on the rear fuselage in Black. These aircraft have been used in combat and reportedly launched AS-5 missiles against targets in Israel during the Yom Kippur war.

Iraqi Air Force Tu-16 Badger Gs saw combat during the Iran/Iraq War. Badgers were used to conduct at least one bombing raid against Tehran airport and several missile attacks against other Iranian targets.

A pair of Egyptian Badger Gs taxi out for a reconnaissance/training mission. The Badger G had both cruise missile and free fall bombing capability. The Egyptian Badgers carry an unusual camouflage of Sand, Green, and Brown over Light Blue.

This AS-5 Kelt, above its ground handling dolly, has been loaded on the port wing pylon of an Egyptian Air Force Tu-16 Badger G. The missile is overall White with Black numbers and a Blue-Gray radome.

Air-to-Surface Missiles

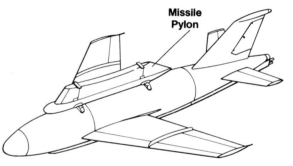

Missile Pylon

**Tu-16K
Badger B
AS-5 Kelt**

Range:	100 miles (Low altitude)
	200 miles (High altitude)
Speed:	Mach 0.9 (Low altitude)
	Mach 1.2 (High altitude)
Warhead:	2,200 pound HE

This Badger G is carrying an AS-6 Kingfish anti-ship cruise missile on the port wing pylon. The two small T shaped antennas under the fuselage are radio altimeter dipole antennas.

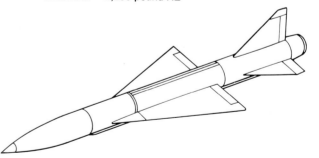

**Tu-16K
Badger G Mod
AS-6 Kingfish**

Range:	135 miles
Speed:	Mach 3
Warhead:	200 kt Nuclear or
	2,200 pound HE

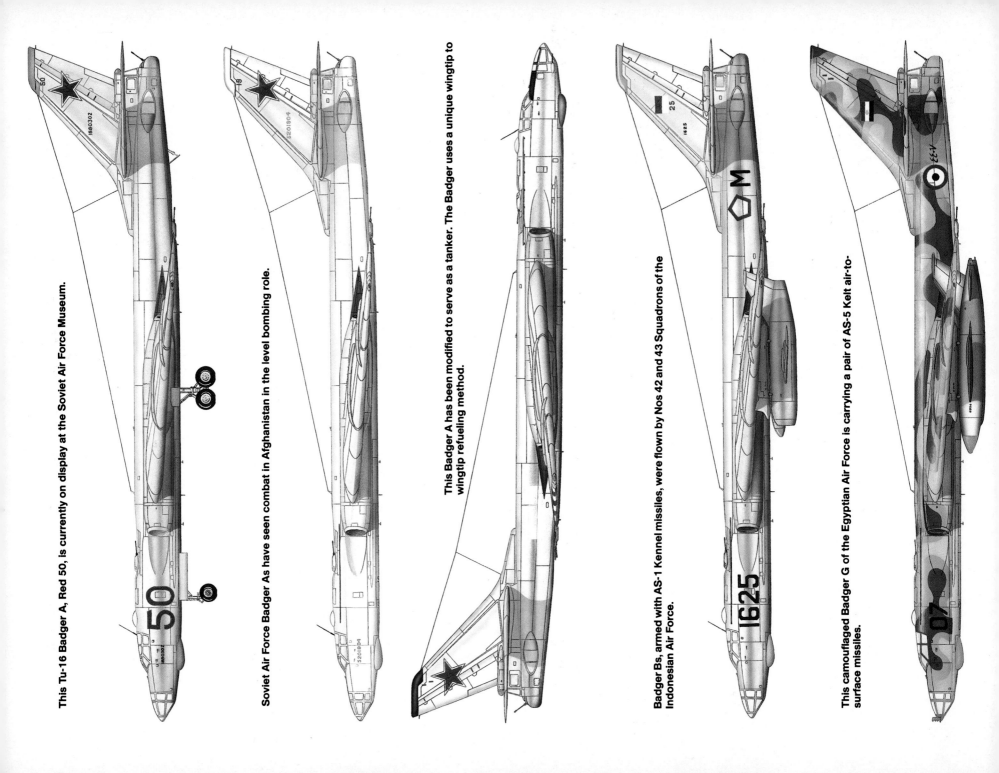

This Tu-16 Badger A, Red 50, is currently on display at the Soviet Air Force Museum.

Soviet Air Force Badger As have seen combat in Afghanistan in the level bombing role.

This Badger A has been modified to serve as a tanker. The Badger uses a unique wingtip to wingtip refueling method.

Badger Bs, armed with AS-1 Kennel missiles, were flown by Nos 42 and 43 Squadrons of the Indonesian Air Force.

This camouflaged Badger G of the Egyptian Air Force is carrying a pair of AS-5 Kelt air-to-surface missiles.

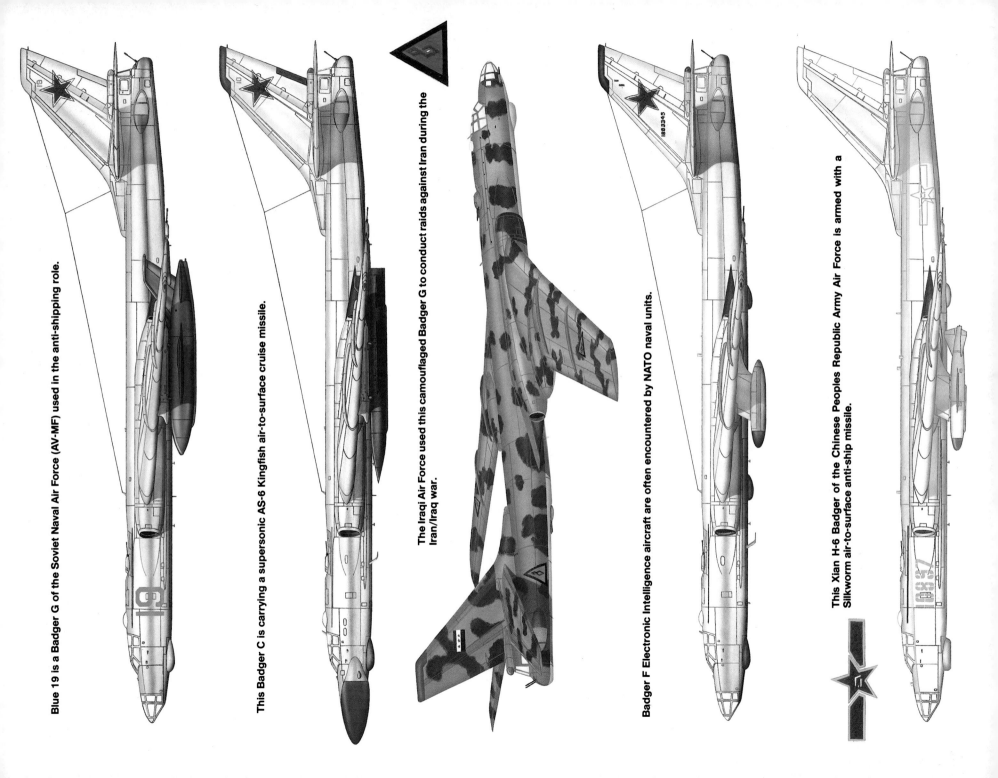

Blue 19 is a Badger G of the Soviet Naval Air Force (AV-MF) used in the anti-shipping role.

This Badger C is carrying a supersonic AS-6 Kingfish air-to-surface cruise missile.

The Iraqi Air Force used this camouflaged Badger G to conduct raids against Iran during the Iran/Iraq war.

Badger F Electronic Intelligence aircraft are often encountered by NATO naval units.

This Xian H-6 Badger of the Chinese Peoples Republic Army Air Force is armed with a Silkworm air-to-surface anti-ship missile.

Fuselage Development

**Tu-16
Badger G**

"T"
Antenna

Short Horn Radar

**Tu-16
Badger G Mod**

"T"
Antenna

Radome
Deleted

Antennas

Blade
Antenna

Radome

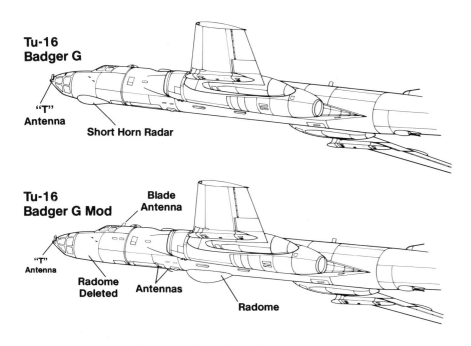

This Badger G Modified has a large teardrop shaped radome under the fuselage that replaced the chin radome of the standard Badger G. It is believed that this radome houses a long range acquisition and guidance radar for the supersonic AS-6.

This Badger G Modified is armed with an AS-6 Kingfish cruise missile on the port pylon. The AS-6 is a supersonic, long range anti-ship missile designed for use against American aircraft carriers.

27

Tu-16 Recon Variants

Tu-16 Badger D

During the early 1960s, the Tu-16 airframe was selected as the best available platform to meet the needs of the Soviet Navy for a dedicated maritime reconnaissance/electronic intelligence (ELINT) aircraft. As a result of this decision, the Tu-16K-10 Badger C was modified for the new mission.

The cruise missile systems were deleted with the missile recess being faired over and three additional blister antennas were added to the fuselage underside. The aircraft was first observed by the West during 1962 and given the NATO reporting name Badger D.

The Badger D differs from the Badger C in having all offensive capability deleted and the addition of three blister fairings for passive electronics antennas installed on the fuselage underside. Additionally, the chin radome under the nose is slightly enlarged. The Badger D serves with the Soviet Navy in the maritime reconnaissance role and also can be used to provide mid-course guidance for missiles launched by other Badgers.

The crew of the Badger D has been increased from six to eight/nine men depending on the special equipment/sensors carried by the aircraft. This increase in crew became common with all electronic/reconnaissance Badgers.

The crew of a Badger D reconnaissance aircraft cross the snow covered ramp after a mission. The forward underfuselage radome is smaller than the radome in the middle of the fuselage. The hatch in front of the nosewheel is the crew entry hatch to the forward compartment.

An F-4B Phantom II of VF-21 off the USS RANGER escorts a pair of Soviet Navy Badgers away from the task group. The aircraft in the background is a Badger D maritime reconnaissance aircraft.

The Badger D is both an electronic reconnaissance aircraft and a long range maritime surveillance aircraft. Reportedly, the Badger D can provide mid-course guidance for cruise missiles launched by other Badgers.

Ground crews service a Badger D. The open hatches on the nose are access panels for the electronic equipment. The Badger D has a slightly larger chin radome than the earlier Badger C.

Fuselage Development

Tu-16 Badger C Mod

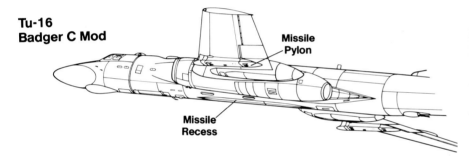

Missile Pylon

Missile Recess

Tu-16 Badger D

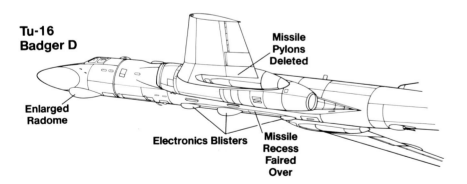

Enlarged Radome

Electronics Blisters

Missile Pylons Deleted

Missile Recess Faired Over

The Badger D has a total of four electronics fairings on the fuselage underside. The first fairing is a radome, while the remaining three are believed to house passive receiver antennas.

A Soviet Naval Aviation long range maritime reconnaissance Badger D. Badger Ds are one of the primary maritime reconnaissance/electronic warfare aircraft used by the Soviet Navy, often working with other variants of the Badger while on patrol.

The Badger D was a conversion of the Badger C missile carrier and shares the same nose radome. The chin radome on the Badger D, however, is slightly larger than the radome used on the earlier Badger C.

The primary identification features of the Badger D Maritime Reconnaisance/Electronic Warfare aircraft are its three ventral electronics blisters/radomes. The blade antennas just in front of the forward radome are communications aerials.

Tu-16R Badger E

All Tu-16s can be used for strike reconnaissance utilizing the vertical camera that is installed in a small compartment just in front of the bomb bay. This camera was intended to provide updating target photographs and for bomb damage assessment and not as a true reconnaissance tool.

To meet the need for a long range reconnaissance aircraft, especially in the maritime role, the Tu-16 airframe was selected and modified to produce a special reconnaissance variant under the designation Tu-16R.

The Tu-16R was introduced into service during the early 1960s and received the NATO reporting name Badger E. It differed from the standard Badger A bomber in having cameras installed on a pallet within the bomb bay along with additional bomb bay fuel tanks. There are two underfuselage blister passive receiver antennas, carried just forward and to the rear of the weapons bay, for electronic reconnaissance duties.

A Royal Air Force F-4 Phantom, armed with a centerline Vulcan cannon pod, flies escort on a Soviet Navy Badger E over the North Sea. The Badger rear guns are in the full up position as a sign of peaceful intent. It is a standing rule that neither aircraft may use the other for a practice target — just in case.

A Marine Corps F/A-18 Hornet keeps close watch on a Soviet Navy Tu-16 Badger E. The Badger E is one of the more commonly encountered Soviet naval aircraft, as they shadow U.S. and NATO naval forces conducting exercises.

A Soviet Navy Tu-16R Badger E electronic warfare aircraft. The Badger is overall natural metal with the radome, fin cap and electronic blisters in Dark Green. The rudder trim tab is in Red.

This AV-MF Badger is engaged on a reconnaissance mission high over the Pacific Ocean. Soviet Navy reconnaissance Badgers have been encountered by U.S. Navy vessels in every ocean from the North Atlantic to the South Pacific.

This overall natural metal Badger E being escorted by a U.S. Navy F-4 Phantom off the USS J.F. KENNEDY is carrying United Arab Republic Air Force (Egypt) markings. These markings were colors of convenience since the Badger was flown by Soviet Navy crews.

UARAF (Soviet crewed) Badgers were a common sight over the Med during the late 1960s and early 1970s. Badgers operating from Egyptian bases could cover nearly the entire eastern end of the Med without refueling.

Fuselage Development

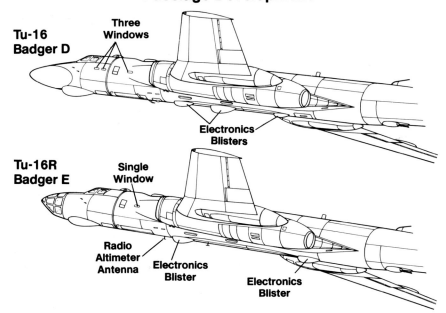

Tu-16 Badger D

Three Windows

Electronics Blisters

Tu-16R Badger E

Single Window

Radio Altimeter Antenna

Electronics Blister

Electronics Blister

The astrodome on this Badger E is manned and there appears to be a camera lens in the fuselage side window. The three pole antenna array on the nose in front of the cockpit is the Odd Rods IFF antenna. The small T shaped antenna is a TW-17 radio altimeter antenna.

The United Arab Republic Air Force (Egypt) insignia consisted of a Red, White, and Black rounded with two Green stars on the White center disk. The insignia was carried on both the upper and lower wings as well as the fuselage sides. The serial number (in Black Arabic style numbers) is 4381.

The single 23ᴍᴍ NR-23 cannon on the nose was fired by the pilot using a PKI gun sight. The two hatches under the nose are crew entry hatches, the forward hatch being used for entry to the glazed nose compartment, while the rear hatch was for entry to the flight deck.

To prevent an incident, Badgers would keep the tail guns locked in the full up position at all times when being escorted. The three small antennas under the fuselage are the rear Odd Rods IFF antenna array. The tail turret ammunition bin has a capacity of 500 rounds of ammunition per gun.

Badger F

In January of 1963, U.S. Navy fighters from the aircraft carrier USS KITTY HAWK (CVA-63) encountered a new reconnaissance variant of the Badger which was given the NATO reporting name Badger F.

Externally the Tu-16R Badger F was similar to the Badger A with the exception of two large electronics pods carried on deep underwing pylons. There are several variants of the Tu-16R in Soviet service, differing only in their avionics, sensors and antenna positions. The large underwing pods are believed to contain passive ELINT (Electronic Intelligence) receivers that are capable of recording, plotting and characterizing enemy radars by their emissions.

In addition to the ELINT pods, the Badger F also has passive receiver blisters on the fuselage underside just forward and just to the rear of the bomb bay. Other Badger Fs do not have these Blisters installed and instead have two large blade antennas mounted on the lower fuselage behind the bomb bay and a small blister just ahead of the bay.

A number of Tu-16R Badger Fs also serve in the electronic warfare role with the additional of an internally mounted noise jammer.

The ELINT pods carried on the Badger F are believed to house passive antennas and recorders that pick up and record radar and other electronic signals. It is believed that the pod used on the Badger F has been specially programmed for use against naval emitters.

In addition to the ELINT pod carried under the wings, the Badger F also has two electronic blisters on the fuselage underside. These blisters house additional passive receiver antennas.

Soviet Navy crewmen prepare their equipment before boarding this Tu-16 Badger F electronic warfare aircraft. These aircraft are conversions of Badger A bomber airframes and retain the nose mounted 23MM cannon.

A crew of a Tu-16R Badger F cross the ramp after a long range reconnaissance mission. The posts on the fuselage side are for the towel-rail HF aerial. The electronic intelligence (ELINT) pods are visible under the wings.

Fuselage Development

Tu-16 Badger A

Tu-16R Badger F

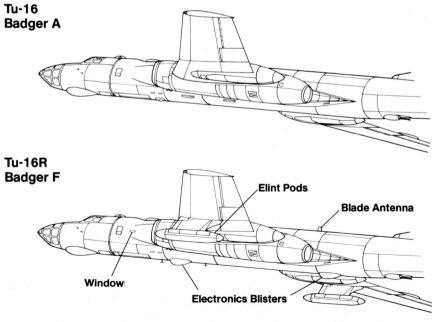

Elint Pods

Blade Antenna

Window

Electronics Blisters

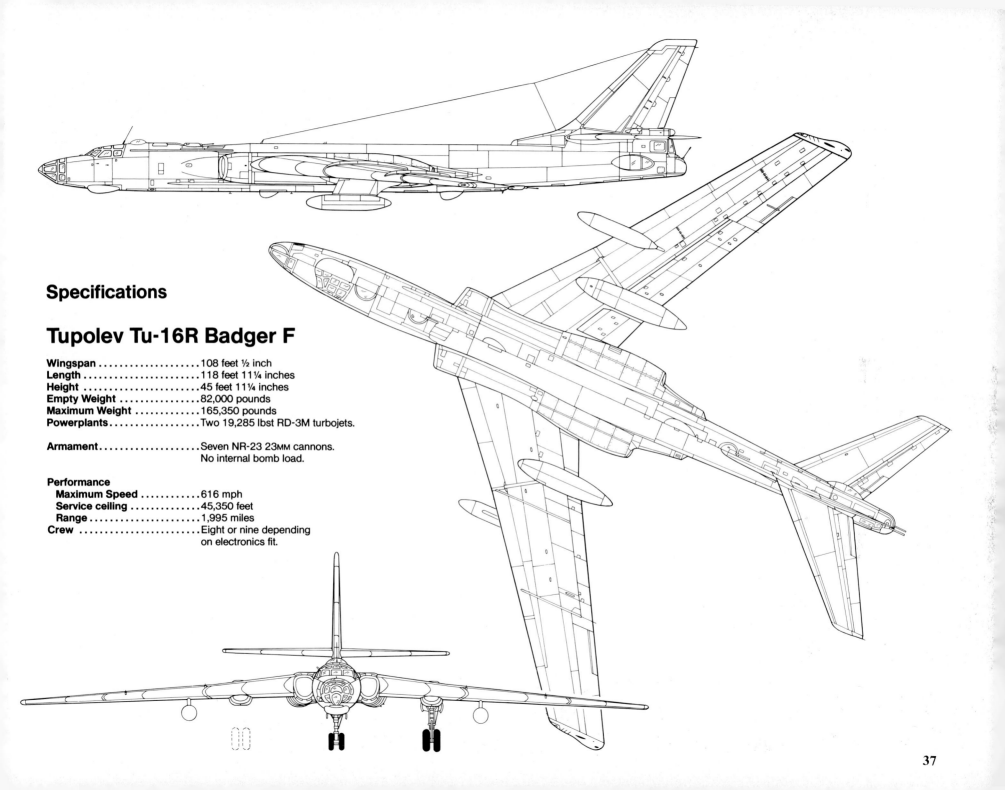

Specifications

Tupolev Tu-16R Badger F

Wingspan . . . . 108 feet ½ inch
Length . . . . 118 feet 11¼ inches
Height . . . . 45 feet 11¼ inches
Empty Weight . . . . 82,000 pounds
Maximum Weight . . . . 165,350 pounds
Powerplants . . . . Two 19,285 lbst RD-3M turbojets.

Armament . . . . Seven NR-23 23мм cannons.
No internal bomb load.

Performance
  Maximum Speed . . . . 616 mph
  Service ceiling . . . . 45,350 feet
  Range . . . . 1,995 miles
Crew . . . . Eight or nine depending
on electronics fit.

A Badger F flies low over the sea near a NATO Naval Task Group. The aircraft carries two electronics pods under the wings which contain receivers for monitoring the electronic signals of radios, radars and other equipment aboard the ships.

This Badger F, being escorted by a U.S. Navy F-14A Tomcat, has been modified with an unusual tail cone replacing the rear 23mm gun turret. The tail cone is similar to ones seen on Tu-142 Bear F, which is used for Extra Low Frequency (ELF) communications.

A Sidewinder missile armed F-4J Phantom escorts a pair of Badger Fs high over the Pacific. It is not uncommon for Badgers to operate in pairs; however, usually they are different variants, such as a Badger E and F.

Although this Badger F carries Egyptian Air Force markings, it was flown by Soviet aircrews. These aircraft were very active over the Mediterranean Sea during the late 1960s and early 1970s. The aircraft have since been returned to the Soviet Union.

A Tu-16R Badger F is escorted by a Sidewinder missile armed F-104G Starfighter of the Royal Norwegian Air Force. North Sea Fleet Badgers are routinely intercepted by Norwegian fighters as they transit around the country enroute to the North Sea.

The main features of the Badger F are the two underwing electronics pods. The Badger F is a long range electronic intelligence (ELINT) aircraft that is often encountered by U.S. Navy units around the world.

This Badger F is carrying United Arab Republic Air Force (Egypt) colors of convenience. These aircraft were later returned to the Soviet Union and were never actually carried as part of the Egyptian Air Force inventory.

This Badger F has been modified with additional sensor antennas over the cockpit on short pylons on the nose and just behind the cockpit.

There is a new Electronic Counter Measures (ECM) antenna just above the Bee Hind gun laying radar radome on this Badger F. This blister probably houses a radar warning receiver antenna.

Besides the new sensor blisters above the cockpit, this Badger F has an electronics blister on a short pylon alongside the nose and a new shaped blade antenna just behind the cockpit.

41

Tu-16PP Badger H

To provide for electronic jammer escort of strike forces, primarily missile carrying Badgers, an electronic counter measures (ECM) variant was designed under the designation Tu-16PP (*postanevshchik pomiekh*). The Tu-16PP Badger H was a specialized chaff aircraft, capable of carrying up to 9,000 kg (19,840 pounds) of aluminum chaff strips in special containers carried in the bomb bay.

The chaff strips are cut into sections of different lengths just before they are dropped. The strips should have a length of one-half the radar wavelength of the station which is to be jammed. In order to accomplish this, the Tu-16PP has one tear drop shaped passive antenna blister just in front of the bomb bay doors and another tear drop blister on the bomb bay doors near the rear portion of the bay. A third small blister is carried immediately in front of the bomb bay. These blister antennas house passive receivers that cover the expected radar frequency range to be encountered. They are used to pick up the enemy radar signals, identify them and establish the proper length of the chaff strips. A large dispenser hatch is located just behind the bomb bay.

Badger H aircraft would normally be used to accompany a strike force and provide protection from surface-to-air missiles and enemy fighter direction radars.

Antenna Configuration

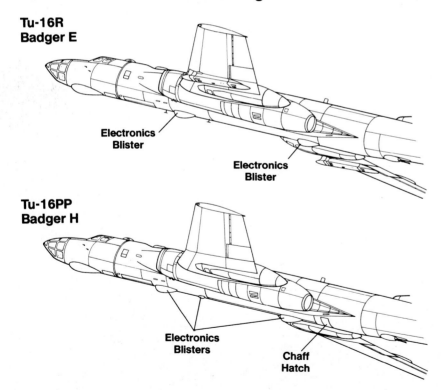

**Tu-16R
Badger E**

Electronics
Blister

Electronics
Blister

**Tu-16PP
Badger H**

Electronics
Blisters

Chaff
Hatch

The Badger H Electronic Counter Measures (ECM) aircraft has two ventral radomes. This variant also carries chaff which is dropped from the hatch visible just to the rear of the weapons bay. The Badger H is an escort aircraft used to protect the missile carrying strike force.

Tu-16PP Badger J

An active electronic warfare variant of the Badger was first identified during late 1987 and given the NATO reporting name Badger J. Although externally similar to the Badger E, this ECM variant was built to perform the active, rather than passive, radar jamming role. For this mission the Tu-16PP Badger J carries high power barrage, click, spot and noise jammers in the weapons bay with the antennas mounted in a long canoe fairing which protrudes from the weapons bay.

Additionally, the aircraft carries large flat plate type antennas mounted on each wingtip and small wingtip pods for other antennas. It is known that some of the onboard noise jammers operate in the A to I frequency bands. There are also several additional blade antennas carried on the upper fuselage, probably for communications equipment.

The jammer installation has its own cooling system and the underside of the fuselage has several heat exchangers mounted alongside the antenna canoe and exhaust ports mounted just to the rear of the antenna canoe.

A number of Badger J aircraft were deployed to the former U.S. base at Cam Ranh Bay in Vietnam and were used to fly patrols over the South China Sea near the Philippines.

An F-4S Phantom II of VF-161 aboard USS MIDWAY escorts a Tu-16 Badger J electronic warfare aircraft as it makes a low pass near the MIDWAY battle group. There are strict rules governing both the escort and the aircraft being escorted, to avoid accidents.

The canoe shaped radome protruding from the bomb bay doors is the distinctive feature of the Tu-16PP Badger J Electronic Counter Measures (ECM) jammer aircraft. This aircraft also carries two flat antennas, one on each wingtip.

The Tu-16PP Badger J is a specialized ECM jammer aircraft built from the Badger A airframe. In combat the aircraft would accompany formations of Badger missile carriers to protect them from hostile radars.

Antenna Configuration

Tu-16PP Badger H

Electronics Blisters

Chaff Hatch

Tu-16PP Badger J

Electronics Blister

Jammer Antenna Canoe

Cooling Vents/Exhausts

Tu-16R Badger K

The most recent variant of electronic reconnaissance Badgers was first identified during 1981 and assigned the NATO reporting name Badger K. Externally similar to the earlier Badger E, it is equipped with two passive electronics blisters just in front of and just behind the bomb bay. The Badger K also has a large window on the port fuselage side just forward of the standard fuselage window. It is believed that this window houses an oblique camera installation.

Most Badger Ks also have a deeper, flatter chin radome and several new blade antennas on the upper fuselage behind the cockpit.

The Badger K is the latest reconnaissance variant of the Tu-16. Externally it is almost identical to the Badger E and Badger H and shares the same electronic warfare mission with both of the earlier variants.

One of the differences between the Tu-16 Badger K and the earlier Badger E are the additional blade antennas above the cockpit. The three dipole antennas on the nose in front of the cockpit are the antenna array for the Odd Rods IFF system.

The Tu-16 Badger K has a larger, flatter chin radome than the Badger E. Both the Badger E and Badger K are electronic reconnaissance/counter measures aircraft carrying active and passive electronic sensors.

One of the differences between the Badger E and Badger K was the large window carried on the port fuselage side between the cockpit and the engine air intake. It is believed that this window was intended to house an oblique camera.

Antenna Configuration

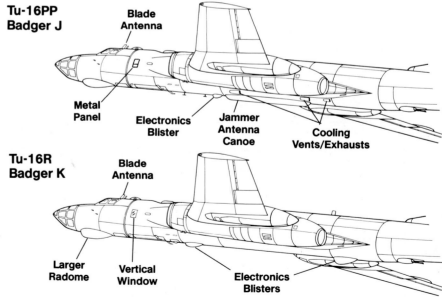

Tu-16PP Badger J

Blade Antenna

Metal Panel

Electronics Blister

Jammer Antenna Canoe

Cooling Vents/Exhausts

Tu-16R Badger K

Blade Antenna

Larger Radome

Vertical Window

Electronics Blisters

Tu-16 Badger L

Recently, a further modification to the Tu-16 airframe has been identified and given the unofficial designation Badger L. During August of 1986, the Soviet aviation magazine "Aviation and Cosmonautics" published a photograph of a Tu-16 in service with the Naval Air Force (AV-MF). This Badger differed from earlier variants in a number of ways. There was a new thimble type radome added to the extreme end of the nose above the bombadier's compartment, the chin radome was larger and flatter, and there was a large blade antenna above the cockpit.

Other modifications included the addition of several small electronics blisters under the nose and on short pylons on the fuselage sides near the air intakes. There are also two underwing pods carried on short pylons. Although not positively identified, it is believed that these pods are chaff/flare self protection jammers. The aircraft also carried an unusual color scheme for a Badger, being Natural Metal over Gloss White.

(Right)
This Badger K reconnaissance variant has numerous small electronics blisters under the fuselage, under the glazed nose and next to the air intake. The aircraft carries both the Excellent Aircraft award and tactical number on the nosewheel doors. The aircraft is Natural Metal over White.

(Bottom Right)
This aircraft has the unofficial designation Badger L. It has been modified with a small thimble radome mounted on the nose and a blade antenna over the cockpit. The aircraft is Natural Metal over White and carries an Excellent Aircraft award on the nose in Red.

Antenna Configuration

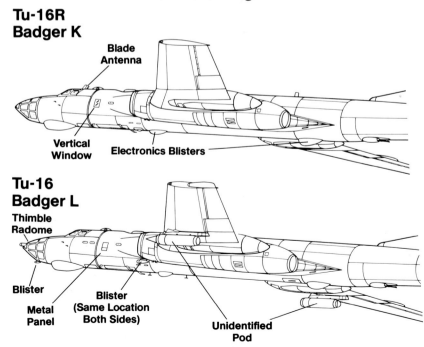

Tu-16R Badger K

- Blade Antenna
- Vertical Window
- Electronics Blisters

Tu-16 Badger L

- Thimble Radome
- Blister
- Metal Panel
- Blister (Same Location Both Sides)
- Unidentified Pod

47

This Badger variant has been unofficially designated the Badger L. Besides the thimble radome on the nose, the aircraft has a number of other features in common with late model Tu-142 Bear anti-submarine/maritime reconnaissance aircraft. The two unidentified pods on the short underwing pylons are identical to those seen on Bear. It is believed that these pods are self protection chaff/flare dispensers. Also in common with Bear Gs are the small electronic blisters near the intakes.

Chinese Badgers

The Soviet Union first supplied China with the Tu-16 during 1958 just before military cooperation and other ties between the two countries was broken off. Part of the disagreement between the two countries centered over the aggressive stand China had taken against Taiwan. Under the protection of the Russian atomic umbrella, China had undertaken military efforts against Taiwan that stopped just short of invasion. The Soviet refusal to transfer nuclear technology to China helped to harden the rift between the two countries.

The Chinese had planned to undertake license production of the Tu-16, however, and had received several pattern aircraft. Without Soviet technical assistance, they were forced to use the same method the Soviets had used with the B-29 — copy and reverse engineer the few aircraft that had been delivered.

The Chinese reverse engineered version of the Tu-16 is built at Xian under the designation H-6 (Hongzhaji bomber 6). This designation is frequently westernized in various publications as the B-6. Chinese variants are also designated by NATO as the Badger, although no separate letter designator has been applied to them. The copied RD-3M engine received the Chinese designation Wopen-8 (WP-8).

The H-6 has become a powerful element of the Chinese Peoples Liberation Army Air Force and during May of 1966 an H-6 dropped the third Chinese atomic bomb during that series of bomb tests. The first production H-6s was delivered during 1968, some ten years after the first Tu-16 entered Chinese service. Subsequent production has continued at a slow pace with an estimated total production of 120 aircraft as of 1987.

The majority of H-6s produced are level bombers, although there are unconfirmed reports of reconnaissance, electronic warfare and tanker versions. During the May 1965 Paris Salon, the Chinese Foreign Trade Office (CPIMEC) offered a new version of the H-6 designated the H-6 IV (B-6D). This aircraft is a cruise missile carrier armed with two C-601 (NATO reporting name Silkworm) anti-ship cruise missiles carried on large under wing pylons.

These missiles are copies of the Russian R-15 (NATO reporting name SS-N-2 Styx), a surface-to-surface anti-ship missile normally carried on surface ships or launched from prepared coastal defense shore sites. These weapons were supplied to the Chinese during the late 1950s and served as the starting point for development of the C-601 air launched Silkworm anti-ship cruise missile.

The H-6 IV Badger differs from Soviet missile carriers in having different shaped underwing pylons and a deeper, flat bottomed radome in place of the chin radome of the bomber variant. There are reports that a number of H-6 IVs have been sold to Iraq with a quantity of C-601 Silkworm missiles. China is also the primary supplier of Tu-16/H-6 spare parts for the Egyptian Air Force, enabling the Egyptians to maintain their Badger Gs without Soviet assistance.

This pair of Xian H-6 bombers of the Chinese Air Force are Natural Metal over White and carry low visibility Gray national insignia on the fuselage sides. The aircraft serial number on the nose is in Blue and the wing insignia is in full color (Red and Yellow).

C-601 Silkworm Cruise Missile

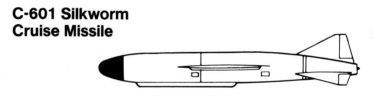

An Xian H-6 IV armed with two C-601 Silkworm anti-ship cruise missiles on underwing pylons. This variant of the H-6 has a larger radome under the forward fuselage which houses the missile guidance radar.

Russian Air Power

1083

1090

6562

...from squadron/signal

1101